Published simultaneously in 1994 by Exley Publications
in Great Britain, and Exley Giftbooks in the USA.
12 11 10 9 8 7 6 5 4 3

Selection and arrangement © Helen Exley 1994
ISBN 1-85015-316-7

Edited by Helen Exley.
Text researched by Margaret Montgomery.
Designed by Pinpoint Design.
Picture research P. A. Goldberg & J. M. Clift/Image Select.
Typeset by Delta, Watford.
Printed and bound by Oriental Press, UAE.
Exley Publications Ltd, 16 Chalk Hill, Watford, Herts WD1 4BN, UK.
Exley Giftbooks, 232 Madison Avenue, Suite 1206, New York, NY 10016, USA.

Text acknowledgements: HRH Prince Charles: extracts from *The Prince of Wales Watercolours*,
Little, Brown, 1991; Winston S. Churchill: extracts from Painting as a Pastime, Penguin, 1964;
Francis Hoyland: extracts from *A Painter's Diary*, Educational Explorers, 1967; Mervyn Levy:
extracts from *Painting For All*, © Odhams Press, 1958.
Exley Publications is very grateful to the following individuals and organizations for permission to
reproduce their pictures: Archiv Für Kunst (AKG), The Bridgeman Art Library (BAL), Fine Art
Photographic Library (FAP), Giraudon (Gir), Scala (Sc), Zefa (Z).
Front cover: (AKG) John Singer Sargent, "Claude Monet painting on the edge of the forest",
Tate Gallery, London; Back cover: (Sc) Ciardi Giuseppe, "Self-portrait at the Easel", Galleria
degli Uffizi, Florence; page 5 (Title page): (Z) Vincent van Gogh; page 6/7: (BAL) Los Angeles
County Museum of Art; page 9: (Gir) Musées Royaux des Beaux-Arts, Paris; page 10: (BAL)
Brooklyn Museum, New York; page 12/13: (FAP) Galerie George; page 14: (BAL) The Fine Art
Society, London; page 16: (Gir) Musée Roubaix; page 17: (Gir) Musée Roubaix; page 19: (BAL) Private
Collection; page 20/21: (Sc) Louvre, Paris; page 22: (AKG) Nationalgalerie; page 24: (Gir/BAL)
Louvre, Paris; page 26: (Gir); page 28: (Gir) Musées Royaux des Beaux-Arts, Paris; page 30/31:
(BAL) © 1994 Gustave François (1883-1963), "The Auction Room at Galerie Georges-Petit,
Paris" (detail), Rafael Valls Gallery, London; page 32: (Gir) Musée Roubaix; page 34: (Sc)
Galleria d'Arte Moderna; page 36/37: (FAP) © 1994 Hans Andersen Brendekilde (1857-1942),
"Big Neels is going to be painted" (detail); page 39: (BAL) © 1994 Dorothea M. S. Johnson,
"Rest time in the Life Class", City of Edinburgh Museums page 42/43: (Gir); page 45: (BAL)
Reading University, Berkshire; page 46: (Gir) Musée d'Orsay, Paris; page 49: (Sc) Jeu de
Paume, Paris; page 51: (AKG) Museum der Bildenden Kunste, Leipzig; page 52/53: (BAL) ©
1994 Lincoln Seligman, "Pigment Jars", Private Collection; page 55: (Gir) Musée Carnavalet,
Paris; page 56: (AKG) Musées Royaux des Beaux-Arts, Paris; page 58/59: (BAL) Victoria &
Albert Museum, London; page 61: (BAL) Spink & Son, London.

ART

Lovers

Quotations

EDITED BY HELEN EXLEY

EXLEY
NEW YORK • WATFORD, UK

"The artist is the person
who makes life more
interesting or beautiful,
more understandable
or mysterious, or probably,
in the best sense,
more wonderful."
GEORGE BELLOWS
(1882-1925)

"Colour is my day-long obsession, joy and torment."
CLAUDE MONET (1840-1926)

❧

"Colour has taken hold of me; no longer do I have to chase after it. I know that it has hold of me for ever. That is the significance of this blessed moment. Colour and I are one. I am a painter."
PAUL KLEE (1879-1940),
on his return from Tunis, 1914

❧

"When it is dark, it seems to me as if I were dying, and I can't think any more."
CLAUDE MONET (1840-1926)

❧

"The purest and most thoughtful minds are those which love colour the most."
JOHN RUSKIN (1819-1900),
from *The Stones of Venice*

❧

PREVIOUS PAGE: CLAUDE MONET, "BLANCHE MONET PAINTING"
OPPOSITE: VALLES, "THE ARTIST'S STUDIO"

John Singer Sargent, "Paul Helleu painting and his Wife"

"The day is coming when a single carrot, freshly observed, will set off a revolution."
PAUL CÉZANNE (1839-1906)

෴

"If we study Japanese art, we see a man who is undoubtedly wise, philosophic and intelligent, who spends his time doing what? In studying the distance between the earth and the moon? No. In studying Bismarck's policy? No. He studies a single blade of grass."
VINCENT VAN GOGH (1853-1890)

෴

"The faculty of creating is never given to us all by itself. It always goes hand in hand with the gift of observation. And the true creator may be recognized by his ability to find about him, in the commonest and humblest thing, items worthy of note."
IGOR STRAVINSKY (1882-1971)

෴

OVERLEAF: PASCALE BOUVERET, "AN ARTIST IN HIS STUDIO"

"Art happens – no hovel
is safe from it, no
prince may depend upon it,
the vastest intelligence
cannot bring it about."
JAMES MCNEILL WHISTLER
(1834-1903)

SKETCH FOR LARGE PICTURE

LAVERY 1883

"Light – dews – breezes – bloom – and freshness; not one of which...has yet been perfected on the canvas of any painter in the world."
JOHN CONSTABLE (1776-1837),
on his aims

∾

"Art is the unceasing effort to compete with the beauty of flowers – and never succeeding."
MARC CHAGALL (1889-1985)

∾

"You come to nature with all your theories, and she knocks them all flat."
PIERRE AUGUSTE RENOIR (1841-1919)

∾

"To any artist worthy of the name, all in nature is beautiful, because his eyes, fearlessly accepting all exterior truth, read there, as in an open book, all the inner truth."
AUGUSTE RODIN (1840-1917)

∾

SIR JOHN LAVERY, STUDY FOR "A PUPIL OF MINE"

"For sheer excitement you can keep movie premières and roller-coasters. An empty white canvas waiting to be filled. That's the thing."
PAM BROWN, b.1928

෨

"...such indeed is the activity of painting: a thrilling tussle between the artist's materials and his inspiration in the course of which an intrinsic part of the whole delicious, exuberant fun, and joy of painting consists in simply not having to bother about making a mess, either of one's person, or of the surroundings in which one is at work."
MERVYN LEVY,
from *Painting For All*

෨

"Just to paint is great fun. The colours are lovely to look at and delicious to squeeze out. Matching them, however crudely, with what you see is fascinating and absolutely absorbing."
WINSTON S. CHURCHILL (1874-1965),
from *Painting as a Pastime*

෨

R. COGGHE, "THE MODEL RESTING"

"...armed with a paint-box, one cannot be bored, one cannot be left at a loose end, one cannot 'have several days on one's hands'. Good gracious! what there is to admire and how little time there is to see it in! For the first time one begins to envy Methuselah."
WINSTON S. CHURCHILL (1874-1965),
from *Painting as a Pastime*

"This was one of those special occasions when I could actually feel the inner appreciation of the beauty of the moment passing like an electric current through the brush in my hand. I was totally absorbed. I was in another world, or another dimension; all sense of time evaporated."
H.R.H. PRINCE CHARLES, b.1948,
from *H.R.H. The Prince of Wales Watercolours*

"When I get my hands on painting materials I don't give a damn about other people's painting: life and me, me and life. In art, every generation must start again afresh."
MAURICE DE VLAMINCK (1876-1958)

OVERLEAF: GIUSEPPE CASTIGLIONE, "VIEW OF THE SALON CARRE"

ABRAHAM SOLOMON, "THE FAIR AMATEUR"

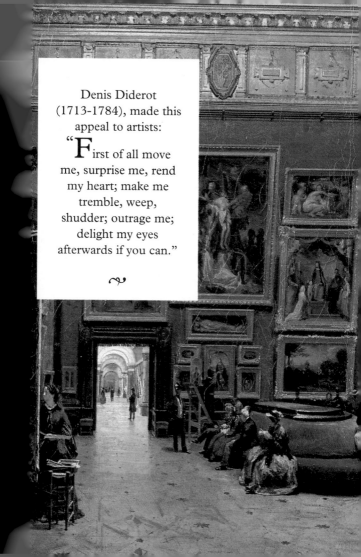

Denis Diderot
(1713-1784), made this
appeal to artists:

"First of all move
me, surprise me, rend
my heart; make me
tremble, weep,
shudder; outrage me;
delight my eyes
afterwards if you can."

༄

"...the real artist while he paints does not think of the sale, only of the need to make a beautiful living thing."
IRVING STONE (1903-1989), fictional Pissarro, from *Depths of Glory*

∾

"To the artist his work is an absorbing passion. He keeps no union hours, he does not ask for vacations, and again and again he has worked without pay and with the most limited recognition."
LOCKIE PARKER

∾

"The true artist will let his wife starve, his children go barefoot, his mother drudge for his living at seventy, sooner than work at anything but his art."
GEORGE BERNARD SHAW (1856-1950)

∾

"The artist needs but a roof, a crust of bread, and his easel, and all the rest God gives him in abundance. He must live to paint and not paint to live."
ALBERT PINKHAM RYDER (1847-1917)

∾

CASPAR DAVID FRIEDRICH, "CASPAR DAVID FRIEDRICH IN HIS STUDIO"

"**P**eople don't realize what they have when they own a picture by me. Each picture is a phial with my blood. That is what has gone into it."
PABLO PICASSO (1881-1973)

~

"In the last analysis, probably the only convincing proof that we can offer to the skeptical of the worth of art, of the reality of its existence and its profound satisfactions, is the fact that men have lived who have willingly foregone social approval, comfort, economic security, worldly advancement, for that long spiritual struggle which is the life of the artist – such men as Van Gogh, Gauguin, Beethoven. These are the names of a few who, living in poverty and obscurity, were yet reclaimed by posterity and canonized."
LOCKIE PARKER

~

"The words 'love of art' are scarcely applicable to him [Van Gogh]; one ought to say: belief unto martyrdom."
PAUL GACHET
(Van Gogh's physician)

~

GUSTAVE COURBET, "THE STUDIO"

"To have taken up painting, no matter at what age, or point in one's life, is to have entered into a new, and deeper awareness of the whole meaning of existence, to have tasted spiritual refreshment, and to have found the perfect form of creative relaxation."

MERVYN LEVY,
from *Painting For All*

∾

"When I begin painting I am in a state of unconsciousness; I suddenly forget that I am holding a brush in my hand."

WU CHÊN (1280-1354)

∾

"It [painting] all requires the most intense concentration and, consequently, is one of the most relaxing and therapeutic exercises I know. In fact, in my case, I find it transports me into another dimension which, quite literally, refreshes parts of the soul which other activities can't reach...."

H.R.H. PRINCE CHARLES, b.1948,
from *H.R.H. The Prince of Wales Watercolours*

∾

Y. BRAYER, "THE BAUX STUDIO IN THE COUNTRY" (DETAIL)

"It seems to me that if any one doubts the value or 'use'
of painting they doubt the value of being. We all
struggle to become as real as possible – to be as
intensely as possible.
Painting is a means by which certain great
people in the past have attained to a maximum
of being and selfawareness, and we can increase
our own reality by the contemplation of their
works – partly because it extends our range of sensations
and partly because of the spiritual content that lies
hidden within these sensations."
FRANCIS HOYLAND,
from *A Painter's Diary*

MULLER, "SELF-PORTRAIT"

"Don't everlastingly read messages into paintings – there's the Daisy – you don't rave over or read messages into it – you just look at that bully little flower – isn't that enough!"
JOHN MARIN (1872-1953)

༙

"A highbrow is the kind of person who looks at a sausage and thinks of Picasso."
SIR A.P. HERBERT (1890-1971)

༙

"*Painting:* the art of protecting flat surfaces from the weather and exposing them to the critic."
AMBROSE BIERCE (1842-1914), from *The Devil's Dictionary*

༙

"If your man says of some picture 'Yes, but what does it mean?' ask him, and keep on asking him, what his carpet means, or the circular patterns on his rubber shoe-soles. Make him lift up his foot and look at them."
STEPHEN POTTER (1900-1969), from *One-upmanship*

༙

OVERLEAF: GUSTAVE FRANÇOIS, "THE AUCTION ROOM AT GALERIE GEORGES-PETIT, PARIS"

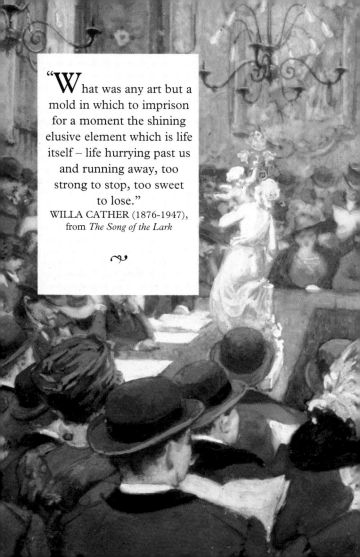

"What was any art but a mold in which to imprison for a moment the shining elusive element which is life itself – life hurrying past us and running away, too strong to stop, too sweet to lose."
WILLA CATHER (1876-1947), from *The Song of the Lark*

"...again and again I've taken quick glances and then for some reason I've got to sit before a picture waiting and it's opened up like one of those Japanese flowers that you put into water and something I thought wasn't worth more than a casual, respectful glance begins to open up depth after depth of meaning."
SISTER WENDY BECKETT,
from an interview on *BBC Radio 2*, 1994

∼

"The true work of art continues to unfold and create within the personality of the spectator. It is a continuous *coming into being.*"
MERVYN LEVY,
from *Painting For All*

∼

"At 5' 3" the only way I am going to see the great paintings of the world is after I am dead – and I can have all the galleries to myself in off-peak hours. The trouble is – there are several million art lovers dreaming the same dream."
PAM BROWN, b.1928

∼

R. COGGHE, "VISIT TO THE MUSEUM"

SILVESTRO LEGA, "VISIT TO THE STUDIO"

"**I** think the experiential test of whether this art
is great or good, or minor or abysmal is the effect it
has on your own sense of the world and of yourself.
Great art changes you."
SISTER WENDY BECKETT,
from *BBC Radio 2*, 1994

༈

"We incline to think that a great painting is like an
earthquake – something that makes itself felt at once
and over a wide area – whereas it could be better likened
to a murder or an act of love: a private episode that may
be discovered 20 years later or not at all."
JOHN RUSSELL,
from *The Meanings of Modern Art*

༈

"A drawing or painting can appeal across the barriers of
time and space with a language of its own – direct,
immediate and alive."
JANET ALLEN and JOHN HOLDEN,
from *The Home Artist*

༈

OVERLEAF: HANS ANDERSEN BRENDEKILDE , "BIG NEELS IS GOING TO BE PAINTED"

"It is art that *makes* life,
makes interest, makes
importance...and I
know of no substitute
whatever for the
force and beauty
of its process."
HENRY JAMES
(1843-1916),
a letter to H.G. Wells,
July 10, 1915

"**H**ave you ever seen an inch worm crawl up a leaf or twig, and then clinging to the very end, revolve in the air, feeling for something to reach something? That's like me. I am trying to find something out there beyond the place on which I have a footing."
ALBERT PINKHAM RYDER (1847-1917)

༎

"Abstract Art has come into being as a necessary expression of the feelings and thoughts of our age; it has added new dimensions to creative painting; it is part of the constant change and vital searching that energizes every true art."
LEONARD BROOKS,
from *Painting and Understanding Abstract Art*

༎

"It's always necessary to seek for perfection. Obviously, for us, this word no longer has the same meaning. To me, it means: from one canvas to the next, always go further, further...."
PABLO PICASSO (1881-1973)

༎

DOROTHEA M. S. JOHNSON, "REST TIME IN THE LIFE CLASS"

"**S**ketching is the *breath* of art: it is the most refreshing
of all the more impulsive forms of creative
self-expression and, as such, it should be as free,
and happy, as a song in the bath."
MERVYN LEVY,
from *Painting For All*

∾

"Art provides us with a pleasing background which
makes living more gracious; it offers a mode of escape
from the troubles and limitations...and now and then it
gives that particular emotion, ecstasy, which is of so
priceless a quality that there is no standard by which to
measure it, one of those rare emotions which redeem life
from monotony, triviality and futility."
LOCKIE PARKER,
from *Art and People*

∾

"I paint as a bird sings."
CLAUDE MONET (1840-1926)

∾

OVERLEAF: Y. BRAYER, "THE BAUX STUDIO IN THE COUNTRY"

ROBERT, "THE MAIN GALLERY OF THE LOUVRE, 1801"

"Art's a staple. Like bread or wine or a warm coat in winter. Those who think it is a luxury have only a fragment of a mind. Man's spirit grows hungry for art in the same way his stomach growls for food...."
IRVING STONE

"An artist's working life is marked by intensive application and intense discipline."
JOHN F. KENNEDY (1917-1963)

❧

"...great art is not a matter of a few virtuosi of the first rank. It is the result of the labours of thousands of faithful craftsmen who know that they are doomed to remain for ever outside the gates of the Paradise of Perfection, but who nevertheless will give the very best there is in them because the work they do means more to them than anything else in this world.
They are the real tillers of the soil."
HENDRIK WILLEM VAN LOON,
from *The Arts of Mankind*

❧

[On why he had not married] "I have a wife too many already, namely this art, which harries me incessantly, and my works are my children."
MICHELANGELO (1475-1564)

❧

"I would sooner look for figs on thistles than for the higher attributes of art from one whose ruling motive in its pursuit is money."
ASHER BROWN DURAND (1796-1886)

❧

"Art among a religious race produces relics; among a military one, trophies; among a commercial one, articles of trade."
HENRY FUSELI (1741-1825)

❧

"...I regard it as a waste of time to think *only* of selling: one forgets one's art and exaggerates one's value."
CAMILLE PISSARRO (1830-1903), in a letter to his son, Lucien

❧

"We have become a society where the artist is regarded as a self-indulgent superfluity, and the person who juggles stocks and shares is an essential part of the economy.
We've gone wrong somewhere."
PAM BROWN, b.1928

❧

BAZILLE, "THE BOTIGNOLLES' STUDIO"

"I have always believed, and still believe, that artists who live and work with spiritual values cannot and should not remain indifferent to a conflict in which the highest values of humanity and civilization are at stake."
PABLO PICASSO (1881-1973)

∼

"Art is a staple of mankind.... So urgent, so utterly linked with the pulse of feeling that it becomes the singular sign of life when every other aspect of civilization fails."
JAMAKE HIGHWATER, from *Fodor's Indian America*, 1975

∼

"If [artists] do see fields blue they are deranged, and should go to an asylum. If they only pretend to see them blue, they are criminals and should go to prison."
ADOLF HITLER (1889-1945), from a political rally speech

∼

"The state is not competent in artistic matters.... When the state leaves us free, it will have carried out its duty."
GUSTAVE COURBET (1819-1877),
from a letter to the Minister of Fine Arts

∼

AUGUSTE RENOIR, "PORTRAIT OF BAZILLE"

"A man paints with his brains and not with his hands."
MICHELANGELO (1475-1564)

"It would be a mistake to ascribe this creative power to an inborn talent. In art, the genuine creator is not just a gifted being, but a person who has succeeded in arranging for their appointed end, a complex of activities, of which the work is the outcome. The artist begins with a vision – a creative operation requiring an effort. Creativity takes courage."
HENRI MATISSE (1869-1954)

"A picture is something which requires as much knavery, trickery, and deceit as the perpetration of a crime."
EDGAR DEGAS (1834-1917)

OPPOSITE: HEINZ WAGNER, "IN THE STUDIO"
OVERLEAF: LINCOLN SELIGMAN, "PIGMENT JARS"

"The art of our era is not art, but technology. Today Rembrandt is painting automobiles; Shakespeare is writing research reports; Michelangelo is designing more efficient bank lobbies."

HOWARD SPARKS,
from *The Petrified Truth*, 1969

❧

"A picture is nothing but a bridge between the soul of the artist and that of the spectator."
EUGÈNE DELACROIX (1798-1863)

᠕

"...art is a means of communication by which mind reaches out to mind across great gaps of space and time, as well as across death."
FRANCIS HOYLAND,
from *A Painter's Diary*

᠕

"Now that I am old and infirm I fear I shall no more be able to roam among the beautiful mountains...I wander and meditate only in dreams...landscapes have a material side and a spiritual influence also. I can only paint my pictures and spread my colour over the cloud-topped mountain to transmit for future ages the hidden meaning which lies beyond all description in words."
CHINESE ARTIST (c.A.D.400)

᠕

DAOLLING, "VIEW OF THE CHURCH OF ST. EUSTACHE"

Alfred Stevens, "The Studio"

"**E**very artist dips his brush into his own soul, and paints his own nature into his pictures."
HENRY WARD BEECHER (1813-1887)

෬

"You do not see with the lens of the eye. You see through that, and by means of that, but you see with the soul of the eye."
JOHN RUSKIN (1819-1900)

෬

"It is now an accepted fact that the expression of emotion through painting, whether practised by children, or by adults, is a source of deep psychological satisfaction and, in the adult practitioner, often a key to the release of tension.... It is a system which can also in some measure, even compensate for the lack of emotional fulfilment in human relationships...."
MERVYN LEVY, from *Painting For All*

෬

"Art is accusation, expression, passion."
GUNTER GRASS, b.1927, from *The Tin Drum*

෬

OVERLEAF:
GEORGE SCHARF SNR., "GALLERY OF NEW SOCIETY OF PAINTERS, OLD BOND STREET"

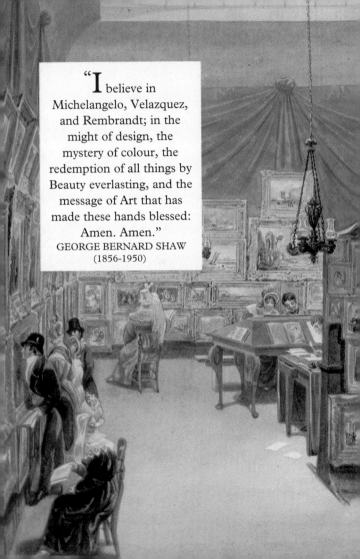

"I believe in Michelangelo, Velazquez, and Rembrandt; in the might of design, the mystery of colour, the redemption of all things by Beauty everlasting, and the message of Art that has made these hands blessed: Amen. Amen."

GEORGE BERNARD SHAW
(1856-1950)

"**W**hen I started to paint I felt transported into a kind of paradise.... In everyday life I was usually bored and vexed.... Starting to paint I felt gloriously free...."
HENRI MATISSE (1869-1954)

∾

"All the sorrows, all the bitternesses, all the sadnesses, I forget them and ignore them in the joy of working."
CAMILLE PISSARRO (1830-1903)

∾

"Creativity is a celebration of life – my celebration of life. It is a bold statement: I am here! I love life! I love me! I can be anything! I can do anything!"
JOSEPH ZINKER

∾

"I hope with all my heart that there will be painting in heaven."
JEAN-BAPTISTE CAMILLE COROT (1796-1875),
his dying words

∾

SIR ALFRED MUNNINGS, "ARTIST PAINTING AT WITHYPOOL"